When Rivers Speak

To Michael Wurster

poet, mentor, critic, friend,
who has been an inspiration
for all my writing projects

When Rivers Speak

James Deahl

UnMon America

Pittsburgh, 2001

Library of Congress Cataloging-in-Publication Data

Deahl, James, 1945–
    When rivers speak / James Deahl.
     p. cm.
    Includes eight poems by Federico García Lorca in English translation by James Deahl.
    ISBN 1-884206-09-3 (pbk.)
    1. García Lorca, Federico, 1898-1936—Translations into English.
    I. García Lorca, Federico, 1898–1936. II. Title.

PR9199.3.D37 W48 2001
811'.54 — dc21

2001046237

Acknowledgements

Some of these poems appeared in the following periodicals: *Cafe Magazine* (U.S.), *Canadian Author* (Canada), *Chapman* (Scotland), *The Endless Mountains Review* (U.S.), *Envoi* (Wales), *First Time* (England), *iota* (England), *Orisha* (Canada), *The Outreach Connection* (Canada), *Poemata* (Canada), *The Spectator* (Canada), *The Tanglewood Trib* (Canada), *Takahe* (New Zealand), *The Windhorse Review* (Canada).

Some of these poems have been read on CHSR-FM radio (Fredericton, Canada) and WYEP-FM radio (Pittsburgh, U.S.)

The following poems have appeared in anthologies:
"On The Death Of An Aged Aunt" in *Small Press Lynx* (Unfinished Monument Press)
"Indigo Bunting" in *Seed* (Bald Eagle Press)
"Prayer For The Dead In September" in *Strong Winds* (Broken Jaw Press)

Many of the poems in the section "Heartland" were initially published in a chapbook of the same name from Envoi Poets Publications, 1993.

UnMon America

(a division of Unfinished Monument Press)
PO Box 4279
Pittsburgh, PA
15203

Unfinished Monument Press is a subsidiary of
Mekler & Deahl, Publishers

Cover and internal illustrations and book and cover design by Gilda Mekler
Printing by Transcontinental

Table of Contents

Songs of Iberia

In The Blue Shadows

The sun is a
bronze gong
hung on the very
edge of our world.

Already the blue evening
is waiting to emerge
from its vineyards.
We have come

to that hour of shadows
when the sea breaks
again and again
with infinite patience

and the sun vanishes
into the west
hungry for night's
dark caress.

The Sea Falls

The sea
falls into the sea
locked in an embrace
        of ecstatic green

beneath tiered
white houses
overlooking the Tejo
that climb
        century by century
these crumbling hills.

Above harbour and city
the copper sun
                lifts
a quay full of gulls
into its burnished eye

while
through the noon heat
a scent of fish
        in hot oil
from shadowed archways

oregano
        and lemon.

Along The Coast

The grey finger
of a lone
lighthouse splits the
living sea
as it journeys
into port.

Tossed below vast
thunderheads
scattered boats fish
the blue hills
of the restless
Atlantic.

Winds race inland
at a string
of bleached orange hills
protecting
their frail village,
and the sea

becomes
a honeycomb
of sound at that
fierce edge where
its great wet hands
flail sharp stone.

Lines Written In Cáceres With Blas de Otero In Mind

Abramos juntos
el último capullo del futuro.

I

All afternoon I heard
the rain's grey voice
drowning in the Rio Almonte.

As the stony ground rose up
like a forehead
inclined to the north

silence filled the spaces
in the rain where
night wished to enter.

II

Near Cáceres
a mother squats at an open fire.

Thin mist and
a field of bitter clay.

She cooks for her family
between the city
and a few brown farms.

III

I sit in a café
where men watch football.

Arabesques of strong tobacco
and sweet coffee,
the score tied at two.

In the blackness
planetrees sparkle,
every leaf jewelled by tears.

IV

Around midnight
the gourd brims fresh with water

and I walk wide boulevards
where palms stir the green air.

It is then,
in the shining dark,
that the prayers of children
finally catch
the elusive ear of God.

V

As rain fills
the red earth

the hopes of Spain
are born anew.

Rushing to embrace its sea
a river opens
the mouth of the night.

Under Serpens

Over the dry hills
of the Sierra de Gredos
olive groves stretch beyond the limits of stone.

The pale leaves silver
their silver night as they ascend
the stairs of darkness along the serpent's tail.

Sparks dance in the eyes
of the viper, dance in black rooms
where silent presses await the living fruit.

The constellation
rises, days of rain and sun lie
as lovers in the green patience of olives.

Ah, the sensuous
longing for that oaken embrace,
for the marble caress of cool white maidens.

I give myself up
to the long black body, lose my
last breath in the cold pulse of the reptile heart.

The autumn deepens.
In our wounded night the pure light
of stars falls drop by drop to the hungry soil.

Canción

In memory of Federico García Lorca

Under the olive branches
Gnarled with the
      strength of earth
A song of Spain arises.

Among red groves of oranges
Stained with their
      naked blood
A song of Spain arises.

In the kernels of dried grain
The arrow
      finds its mark
A song of Spain arises.

By the vineyards of the Penedès
The Black Virgin
      lifts her veil
And a song of Spain arises.

Cada Canción

Every song
is a still place
of love.

Every star,
a still place
of time:
a knot
of time.

And every breath
a still place
of crying.

Paisaje

The field
of olive trees
spreads and shuts
like a fan.
Above this grove —
the deep sky
and its dark rain
of brilliant, icy stars.
Reedbeds tremble
in the half-light of the river;
the grey air ripples.
And the olive trees
stand burdened
with cries.
A flock
of captive birds
preening their long tails
within the deep shadows.

Barrio de Córdoba

Nocturnal Theme

In the house, they hold out
against the stars.
The night collapses.
A lifeless girl lies inside
with a single rose
grown deep within her hair.
Six nightingales sob
from the bars of their prison.

The men sigh
with their guitars open.

Dos Marinos en la Orilla

I

In the passages of his heart
lives a fish from the China Sea.

Sometimes he watches it swim,
tiny, before his eyes.

Because he is a mariner he has forgotten
all the bars and oranges.

He looks out over the waters.

II

With the language of soap
he washes his promise and is silent.

Only one straight world, one curled ocean,
a hundred stars, and his boat.

He has known the Pope at his balcony
and the golden breasts of young Cuban girls.

He looks out over the waters.

Media Luna

The moon journeys through the water.
How tranquil the Heavens!
She slowly harvests
the ancient tremor of the river
while that young frog
leaps boldly into her white mirror.

La Luna Asoma

When the moon comes out
the silent bells
and the impenetrable paths
appear.

When the moon comes out
seas sweep over the earth
and the heart feels
like an island in the infinite.

No one eats oranges
beneath a full moon.
One must have fruit that's
green and cold.

When the moon comes out
the hundred identical faces
on one's silver coins
sob in deep pockets.

Deseo

Only your warm heart,
and nothing more.

My heaven is a country
without nightingales
or lyres;
it contains a discreet river
and a tiny fountain.

It has neither the spur of the wind
over the leaves,
nor the star that longs
to be a petal.

An enormous light
shines outside
wishing to become a glow-worm
in that country
of shattered glances.

It's a clear haven
where our kisses,
richly luminous,
become echoes
opening far in the distance.

And your warm heart,
nothing more.

Encrucijada

The wind of the East,
a lantern,
and the knife
through the heart.
The road
trembles like
a rope
stretched taut,
trembles
like an enormous blowfly.
Everywhere I look:
the knife
through the heart!

The Gift

Prayer For The Dead In September

All evening that bird
has called from his weeping beech,

now the Pleiades pierce the heart of Heaven,
welcome the pain of the first iron frost.

In flowing robes the sisters turn and
return across this harvest earth.

And the dead, so still in their lying down,
seem truly beyond words —

yet words ascend the transfiguring dark.
There are no good-byes,

only a scattering of prayer candles
and the thin grass awaiting

winter's Grace.

Winter Apples

I

One killing frost and the
trees are stripped clean
under a barren sky.

To the north of the road
cold stones read *Grave*, read *Sleep*,
read *Death*

and even that row of
innocent birch
is seduced in silence.

II

Beneath a purple beech
Ukrainian graves,
Russian, Pole — bones

that fought Stalin
lie dense as iron
in their house of clay.

The willow, too, weeps
a purple hunger
where black tongues go.

III

We the living, how shall
we step where our path
rises towards evening?

Among red berries
the mind's cast astray
like winter apples

or the dark breasts
of a girl learning
to become the sea.

Autumn In The Cemetery

After the first cold nights
the maples enter a red fire.

They light up fields
where five generations sleep
in cool white houses.

Through the days of early dark
maple boughs rise ecstatic,

cast their scarlet song
into the deep coolness
of the autumn river.

On The Death Of An Aged Aunt

Wilma Deahl (1910 - 1990)

The winter wind
On a branch outside the window
A single apple.

Against the springhouse
Stalks of frozen wildflowers
Scrape white stone.

Standing in your kitchen
How quickly the darkness comes
As autumn closes.

Unpruned since you left
That yellow rose twists around
The hollow wind.

The garden reclaimed!
Under the roof of the old barn
Swallow nests.

If Only

our lives could stay
at high autumn,
our bodies entwined
throughout the long
cool night.

If only these haws
could remain on their trees,
red lanterns
lighting our path
through early dusk.

Sometimes

Sometimes there is only this dark
and the ravings of rain

at my window.

Towards dawn
those black birds that cried

in the brush all night

arise, fly where the deep
light of the south

lies waiting.

October

We awaken to autumn's
first scattering of snow
and feel our baby move.

With your great round belly
you lean into the cold
to gather our last green tomatoes.

They fill the window sill,
ripen slowly
turning the light to water.

Wild Grapes

Deep in the small hours
our baby turns and turns again
within her sack of water.
Through our bedroom window
I watch Jupiter swing high;

before long Orion will stride into view.
Still she swims
toward this world of things
where each river carries into morning
its own inner grief.

Wild grapes are a song of dark trees.
They shrivel with transparent frost
as starlight falls about them.
Within each purple globe
a frozen sea burns.

The Gift

Labour

The hardest work
is done by women

opening the cervix

that centre point
babies tumble through

belly heaves

thighs turn purple
with excess blood

push down hard

ligaments stretch
even the very bones

move and open

a whole world falling
to new life.

Uterus

It appears to have
a life of its own

the uterus contracts
tightens, forces
our baby's head

into that close space
where thighs open.

Pushing

Bent double
on hands and knees

heavy belly
pressing the mattress

face scarlet, grimaced
every muscle tight

breathe and push
breathe and push

the last inch of
large intestine

turned inside out

trickle of diarrhea
mixed with blood

the great belly churns
and the outside world vanishes

bearing down
inside out

a deep throat sound
black and swollen

breathe and push
push.

Simone

Water girl
swimming grey
          glistening
up into our air

still attached
by the thick blue cord.

A tiny fish
you shimmer
in winter's light —

what were you
          before
you entered our lives?

Already we are changed
          already
you bring
a new life
into ours

a gift
yours to us.

On The Departure Of My Eldest Daughter

Zōsan

Out of autumn mist
mountains

even the fleeting sun
is eaten up.

By the river
drinking wine –

a sound
deep in the sound

of mist.
The day opens

thoughtlessly
like a red pot

swung by tide.

Sesshū

Along the coast
trees lose their colour

as loneliness
fills the heart.

A boat puts out
and the sea expands

endlessly filling the void
with its blue voice.

Hills rise over hills
and we drift

on those dark currents
where the moon

is yet unborn.

Mu-ch'i

Persimmons ripen
in the autumn wind.

The sun
wanders the heavens.

Weightless,
light as a sparrow,

Earth rises
on a wisp of smoke.

We travel
this empty world

our blood also
ripe for the harvest –

a sharp red taste.

Niten

The pine is bristly;
each branch a warrior's sword.

It pulls stars
from the night sky,

lifts the moon
from its warm sea bed.

After centuries of growth,
needles pierce our world

to its fiery core.
Lava rises and

that old crow returns.
By black streams I'll eat

next spring's cold strawberries.

Liang K'ai

With short, brisk strokes
Hui-neng cuts the

bamboo. All attention
placed on the blade,

on the moving edge.
When work is finished

the wind remains
moving the bamboo,

that wooden spirit.
Already your face

is iron and bone.
In a secluded forest

sound of a blade through air.

The Loneliness Of Stones

The sun rises distant and aloof.
People come and go
seeming to enter or leave the room.
All day the table stands in bright sunlight
holding a bowl of fruit.

The business of life occurs.
Tobacco, coffee,
Rachmaninoff's *Symphony in E Minor*
tempt the heart from its cage of flesh.
Children are born in the darkness
between their mother's legs.

And we are all born
from the cry of skin touching,
from that burning,
impossible hunger.

In the evening I consider
the loneliness of stones:
how they come from deep under the earth
only to return
to their primal fire.

A window opens and closes.
The night's last bell strikes home,
its sound entering the black doorways.

The Aroma Of Plums

I

Let us forget about Lorca
and the brutality of the heart.

In Granada a white girl
separates wind from shadow,

a priest enters the darkness
of a café.

II

Let us lie naked as heat
while outside the hotel

the aroma of plums
drifts through afternoon streets

and that small death comes
fresh as the flight of birds.

Forge

Le soleil et ton coeur sont de même matière.

– Pierre Reverdy

Darkness;
thick oak beams and darkness.
The sudden arc of sparks,
a steady thump, thump
of bellows.

Buried in its bed of coke
a star grows,
becomes a vast pulsing
furnace of gas.

Hands, white-knuckled,
scarred
swing the hammer,
clouds of steam
as iron hardens in water.

Iron!
A ring of iron
struck against the anvil –
my naked heart vibrates
in space.

Los Alamos

Le feu jamais ne guérira de nous,
Le feu qui parle notre langue.

— Jacques Dupin

They journey
deeper into the desert,
into that arid juncture
of sun and the dry west wind.

Land of adobe and dust,
of canyons under burning skies.
Every rock wall holds a face,
a memory of events past.

It is not the heat
nor the lack of water
that will kill, but
the expectations of pleasure

forever unfulfilled.
The men advance,
become dust devils
beating on blind stone;

become those who will speak
into the mineral dark
words that may someday
destroy our world.

Prelude To Departure

Already summer is fading;
the final day-lilies twist and fall.
I wait patiently for goldenrod,
forever in its coming.

Today I note
the passage of time,
life's daily cruelties,
the sudden possibility of death.

At midnight I feel the stars move
as their light towers above me.
I open wide,
strain into their blackness.

And the blackness comes.
In the cold hour it enters my pupil,
wells up like the dark canto
of workmen from beyond the tide.

The Wall

A wall of tough stone runs down a slope from the high avenue into the bus depot. Because of this year's unusually hot spring this barrier is dry, entirely without moisture. Even the crevasses where snow would often nest among tiny flakes of broken mortar are empty and baked. The whole grey face is obstinate, dense in its mineral sleep.

Within the structure of this rock, small fragments of granite are locked in a motionless room with quartz and other materials that have spent years on the bottom of our inland sea. I reach out and touch the fierce gravity of the wall, touch its atoms of hard packed silence. A desert, bitter with sun, stretches as far as I can reach. Its scalding winds, although present, cannot be heard. I see nothing but half-buried remains where an important city stood, a few faint clouds high in their pale sky.

In the mouth of the desert it is difficult to remember water. I can hardly recall the caress of a woman or her shy dampness in the bed of love. All around lies grey stone, inflexible as the hand of a proud god whose face is carved from fire. When that hand moves I walk out alone, always alone, into the scorpion wind.

In The Italian Section

Along the hot boulevards
women in miniskirts
       on this first
sunny day
         of spring —

coats thrown open
their legs so white
       from six months of winter
laughing, laughing
         Oh, to be alive!

And yes, to be born anew
in the sun
       on this street of shy girls
from the convent school,
       their thick wool stockings —

and mounds of olives
tomatoes, dark eggplants
       filling the stalls
spilling over the edge
         all we could want.

Market

At the end of a Portuguese street
       set back
behind the row of shops

blue domes of a synagogue
       surrounded by the dust of a city park
some stunted trees –

I buy olives, salty cheese
       thick crusty bread
sit and eat.

The bearded Jews
       have all departed
to new homes, outer suburbs

their synagogue floats awash
       in disco, North African
music, the constant

hubbub of fishmongers
       buying and selling –
smell of garlic, of strong coffee

the market.

Pittsburgh IX

Rivers made this city. Wars made it strong.
Pole, Slav, Ukrainian, Hungarian
washed across the sea on an ebb of blood.
Korea and Vietnam offered jobs
for sons, grandsons; kept Homestead's heart burning
triumphant in its rainbow of hot steel.

The High Level Bridge was an arm of night
reaching bank-to-bank through rank, clotted air.
Above the river's ache and swing our sky
hung spiked on burn-off shot from open hearths.
Shops stayed open, new cars filled bright streets with
gleaming chrome while far away the daily
news of death kept us working, warm, well fed.

Pittsburgh X

Below Westinghouse Bridge stretched the plant where
Uncle George acquired great wealth and father
earned his keep. On Family Days his lightning
snapped from Van de Graaff machines to light the
vast and sullied dream. Thousands worked along
Turtle Creek, their generating station
banishing turtles and all else with heat.

Still every spring until the end was near
that creek snarled through East Pittsburgh grey with rage
tearing sandbags from blind factory doors.
Once I watched it swirl ten feet deep; parked cars
packed tight with slime. Now gutted buildings slump
beside cold waters filled again with life.

After The Darkness

The old Sister on the streetcar
has hands like broken claws,
every knuckle and vein
knotted, enlarged
beneath thin, pale skin.

A massive cross hangs
at her neck. Yet,
as we turn west,
her glasses burn with the blue fire
of August's sun.

It is as if she sees angels
dancing like harvestflies
as they rise above our earth
after three years of darkness.

The Hall Lantern

A heavy tide runs raw
across the shingle, forced on
by a sting of snow slanting
off our comfortless bay.

The year's sharp turning –
dune grass breaks in driving cold
while November's squalls pound
pewter clouds upon a pewter sea.

Along the harbour road we hurry,
past saltbox homes three centuries old.
The hall lantern, the bull's-eye clock
speak of darkness run thick as solder.

Old house of an older season;
we tremble naked with the night
while beyond our bedhead
the moon is blurred by cloud and salt.

The Wisdom Of The Body

for Martha

The body always recalls
what the heart, the mind
let pass.

A brutal summer. Red dust
and the reek of grain elevators
astringent along the waterfront.

In our night's tight core
your breasts rose to black nipples,
your thighs were the
hot wind off the lake.

My fingers trace lines of sweat
along the hidden cunt –
and it's magic

the way the lips open
moist with their scent of night,
the way my blood rises thick
where darkness gathers like stone.

And my hunger
to be taken completely
into your seething flesh.

Not even naked
but the half-slip bunched
about your long muscled waist.

In the narrow cot
brown legs wrap the dark
and I eat you

tongue searching the swollen nerve
till you writhe like a holocaust
as the sharp bud cries
in my flowering mouth.

The heart may attract
but only lust hammers two bodies
into one.

We have become the black opening
of the tide,
become the bowl of cherries
carried cold from the fridge.

Our bodies are consumed.
You silently swallow each crimson sphere
with burning joy.

The Gorge

No quiet brook, but
a torment of water roaring through
cut green rocks to leap
straight into that shattered space where a

crossfire of stones
catches each drop and flings it breakneck
against fern and deadfall.
Not some gentle pool, but a flashing

turban whipped in a
death-knot of foam 'round and 'round between
compassionless rocks
while wrapped in high mist at the cliff's lip

a lone arbutus
clings firm, leaning like a girl counter-
balanced against need
into the white-tossed throat of the gorge.

Bog

Press at any point —
dark water rises high as your wrist,
pushes upward to
keep its green raft buoyant and alive.

At the bog's moist heart
skunk cabbage struggles through moss and sedge
to thrust bright yellow
into a salt-edged gust of sea wind.

From acidic peat
a gnarl of cedar and lodgepole pine
twists stunted against
the fossil sky, brittle as branches

tinged with salt. All day
a squall sweeps in off the Pacific.
It takes a century
to add an inch to a single tree.

In The Green World

In the green depths of
the gorge startled water swirls around
a tumble of rock
to burst green with oxygen into

a rainbow-arched sky.
Oh, I need this green where gloved moss clings
to tangled stone and
glacier-born streams thrash headstrong into

the sea's white skeins, while
in the woods lemon-clouded maples
bud pale green fire in
the darker texture of fir and pine.

I also need that
surprising green of water soaring
in overturned sun
to spill mountain pools of soft green light.

Heartland

The Balance

Like a twig caught
          by an eddy
the Great Bear
          circles Polaris.

Seeing such
          constancy
it's possible to
          imagine paradise –

to imagine stars
          in near vacuum
speaking a tongue
          without sin.

Omnivorous,
          living in blackness,
tiny bonfires
          to steer by,

a path set out
          through dark waters
for sailors to dream
          and follow.

November

Cast-down maple leaves
lie in a yellow pool
spread on thin grass;

the flare of sumac
cresting its hill
is a signal
warning of winter gales.

Already cold winds rise;
leaves dot the river
like distant suns.

On The Prairies

On the Prairies
cold November rains
fall into the open ground.
They shift across fields
where grain once rose
proud in its harvest coat.

From deep porches
farmers scan bleak skies
for signs of the first snow;
and winter comes
redemptive in its purity,
in its sharp steel.

Husk

After the first hard frost
farmers enter upon their frozen land
to bring in the year's feed corn.
Along rough county roads

draught horses plunge in heavy air,
forged shoes striking congealed ruts.
Stalks rustle in the wind's teeth
brittle with the scent of snow.

Through the long dusk the grain
is dragged by solitary workmen
to barns that lean red
into the blood of a harvest sky.

All autumn the men go
silent among the ragged trees that
mark off field from hand-worked field.
Stiff with sleep they dream of corn,

dream of that bullet of frost
lodged in the heart of every kernel,
of the dead weight of each iron
ear in the shucking hands.

Dark Waters

Frost has turned the goldenrod white,
  almost like snow;
the barest flush of early dawn
  lies on the Thames.
On the path to town I watch
  migrating mallards
drift out across the icy water,
  mere ripples of black.
There is no other movement
  just these ducks,
dark dots bobbing on dark waters
  turning the world.

Tanglewood Orchard

I

After weeks of dry weather
snow builds its white house
in the summer bower.

II

Far to the west, quicksilver clouds
blot out our distant sun;
the last leaves rattle their bare trees.

III

Cardinal and blue jay
decorate scrub and hedgerow –
the only colour to touch the woods this season.

IV

I cast out crusts for birds and rodents.
Dark smoke rises into the sunset;
I open the door to the winter.

V

All night going home
the wind carries bits of light
into morning's bright hive.

Hawk

Late November.
A white stillness
          spreads
    field to field

cows wander
    with heavy breath
searching through
              frozen stubble
              for overlooked corn.

    In the cemetery
Loyalist graves
          two centuries old

    the struggle
for harvests,
                  for children,
    for their hard
          cold land.

The winter hawk
    glides
          looking for mice

its rich brown
          is set against
the grey
          of banked storm clouds
stretching
    to Lake Huron
              and beyond.

Into Light

for Shona Rachel Ella Deahl

You are pushed into light by the dark body
as it convulses in its cave of pain.
I hear your thin wail and grunt
as streamers of blood are wiped away and
you are carried off by the midwife
to be weighed and wrapped.

Outside lies the stilled night.
Venus crosses the border into Virgo;
soon snow will streak our sky.
I lift the book and read: "Bestow
Your blessing on our child, that she may grow
in strength of body, mind, and spirit.
May she learn to love all that is good
and beautiful and true."
Goddess of Spring, Goddess of Justice,
seeker of life and truth, whose darkness
will your love-light soften? Whose word
will quicken your heart to compassion
before our nights grow long?

For only death is certain
and we are like mad explorers
trudging further north under winter's triangle.
Yet tears of joy grace every cheek.
In the bright room we form a ring of life,
lurch drunk on sleeplessness
into the luminous folds of a fresh dawn.

A Winter Birth

for Simone Dorothy Reesa Deahl

> *The works of God*
> *are full of providence;*
> *The works of Fortune*
> *are not independent of Nature . . .*
> *Thence flow all things.*
> — Marcus Aurelius

With a twist of forceps
you are delivered into a life
where deliverance, if it comes,
comes with that final dark
far from the bright lights
of this incandescent room.

Though darkness fills
the cracks that edge our days,
we celebrate your first week
by lighting candles,
let the Menorah
illuminate our lives,
a festival of joy in yours.

Home early from work,
I hold you to a window
to catch the last December light,
watch while our sun sets
in its prison of ice.
I know I cannot save you
from life's pain.

All things flow
and you grow into spring.
In green shade I walk
through the fortunate dark
of new buds. I'm shaped
to your stillpoint,
the immense world moving
ponderous around us.

Quite Early Christmas Morning

Quite early Christmas morning
the Herdsman rises in the east
to stand over the stripped branches
of poplar and oak. Below his waist
swings an orange lantern
to light the way for the coming dawn.

The town's shut tight;
the sky between Arcturus and
Spica wears its black mask.
Snow hides in the roots of dark trees
while above the river, mist ghosts
cast halos about the streetlamps.

Wise men have long understood
light consumes the terrors of our night,
and so these constellations
swing above our heads —
each a bright song sung
in darkness waiting.

Witness

Snow swept in today
to bury the browns
of a winter's afternoon.

These are the vast storms
born far in the wheat-lands.
They cross a thousand barren miles
to reach these lowland fields.

A century and a half past
the first Loyalists
entered this valley.

Here they founded an Anglican church,
raised a building
to house an Orange Lodge,
set out their cemetery.

I have seen their stones
leaning white into
the whiteness of Prairie storms.

Poems For A Winter River

I

All day your grey waters carry rafts of ice
to Lake St. Clair and Detroit
as the year closes.

II

In the heart of the marshland
dry reeds whisper their grief
to the winter wind.

III

I wander the river bank
lost in a hundred shades of brown
as bells summon the faithful to mass.

IV

The evening lights
its dark lamp
in an empty heron's nest.

V

I follow the south fork home;
the radiant Twins overhead are unmoved
by the *canto negro* of the river at night.

Winter Dawn

Out of the east
      a cold snow;
in country fields
      lying beneath grey mist
ice flowers bloom
      among dry corn stubble.

The land is open
      and white
pierced only
      by black trees
stripped bare by weeks
      of heavy frost.

The great silence
      of early dawn
covers farm and woodlot
      – even the old rooster
dares not speak
      to the apple tree today.

Tableau

Not a leaf is left
on the poplars
where they stand locked
in their frozen pools.

Behind their boughs
winter turns the sky to silver
as daylight darkens
over an icy river.

Deep in the floodplain
nothing moves
save a man and his dog
silently walking the iron ground.

January Thaw

After a month of snow
an unexpected thaw –
the river rose,

                spilled over
its banks
      all the way to clay bluffs.

The path to town washed out
I stay home,
             watch cold water
swirl through branches
where last week
      black squirrels raced.

A Winter's Day

I

Ice crystals ghost across
sheets of frozen water.
Snow fills the little baskets
of Queen Anne's Lace
with blue silence.

Darkness resides
among bare branches.
The familiar birds
stay in the brush, remain
deep in their animal solitude.

Everywhere sons wait
for the cup to pass.
The fathers have grown old,
they silently gather at the river
of grief, at the river of hope.

II

Winter bulls stamp sullenly
within the lee of stone barns.
Frozen drifts sweep like
a white sea across road
and pasture.

I boil water for tea,
look into the west
as if expecting deliverance.
I wait for snow to melt,
for rivers to freshen.

Downstream, chains of great cities
loom out of farmland.
Men in black stand
at the gates of empire
like convicts awaiting darkness.

III

Our sun flames down wrapped
by winter colours;
darkness gathers along
a frozen river
as the evening star comes.

Beneath its skin of ice
the Thames flows to Lake St. Clair
where another, deeper river
carries the cold of the North
faithfully, without regret.

There can be no salvation
through deeds alone.
The creek lies buried
when winter purifies
the ravine with white hands.

The Walk

I went for a walk today
    across the frozen floodplain
        to the river;
two days after Saint Patrick's day
      and it's mostly thawed
with only a few yards of ice
        lining each bank,
    the water
      slate grey
under
    a slate grey sky.
I turned downstream, toward where the wetlands
      run into the bluffs
and
    the heron nests
      its frog-filled summer long.

But today all is white between clay bluffs and water,
the mullein frozen in its coat of ice
    stands sentinel
      beside its solid creek.
Here the river cuts a switchback around
        some harder rock
and ice plates are trapped by the uneven flow,
rushing downstream only to curve back
    bobbing upstream
      in the arms of a contrary current;
and so the ice plates
complete
    their endless circles,
      no two alike,
each floe jostled by its fellows
in the river's crook.

I watch them swing 'round
                    and 'round again,
white ice in grey water.
A *V* of geese passes overhead.
Finally,
          I turn and return
                         along my footprints
          into the north-east wind;
brown skeletons of goldenrod, Queen Anne's Lace, curled dock
                    rattle above ankle-deep snow.
I startle a goldeneye
          into sudden flight,
check last autumn's high-water mark
          on bank-side willows:
                         higher in the branches than my arm can reach.

I know that soon new dock will sprout
          from heart-blown seeds;
fresh shoots will topple
               last year's brittle goldenrod.
And the blue heron
will fly in
                    from the Gulf of Mexico
          to vie with young boys for minnows at the water's edge.

The geese have gone;
          shadows pool in footprints left in snow.
A sharp wind sings
               in willows
where spring's premature yellow
               already tints branch and bud
to signal
          our slow returning sun.

The Endless Blue

Among leafless trees
         scattered jack pines
go scraggly in wind.
         The brook lies quiet
under its skin
         of ice.

A deepening red
         creeps along the canes
of the raspberries.
         At the edge
of the escarpment
         snow clings to blank rock.

All around me
         a hard clarity.
And I am happy
         for the sharp skies,
for the endless blue
         of heaven.

Cattails

From the shallows, last year's cattails thrust bleached and bitten into the sunset. The millpond has been drained, and I walk among the parchment stems where only last week water stood. Dry heads, stalks, and leaves are the same faded colour; some seeds pull loose, bits of fluff in a slight wind. Beyond each seed-head, a sharp spike points directly at heaven.

These are the few strong ones; they rise from a lake bottom matted thick with their fallen brothers. The defeated ones lie in all directions, some cut down by winter gales off the Great Lakes, others by the relentless force of cold spring floods. The survivors stand resolute like sentinels alert for enemy movements. They are hard facts, stiff in the night. And their seed will rise in resurrection. Brother to brother, they touch in the silence where truth resides.

On The Morning The Flowers Bloomed

On the morning the flowers bloomed
I hurry past the first spring scilla,
scattered without warning across winter's grass,
and am borne away through a train's dark tunnel
to a city where poetry is sold.

All night those blossoms pushed
into our fragile air; now on the blue rim of light
they rise where frost has cast
its long white coat, where pale winds
bury a season's grief.

Summoned by the need of an opening year
flowers dance brightly from this dark earth,
each petal an indelible caress
like the bruise love leaves
where skin lies softly hidden.

Sometimes I dream of loving a woman –
dream of fresh grass, of cool vernal rains.
Our torsos rise, lit by the coming dawn
and our breath sings among young leaves
as they burst green through day's tough bark.

Lighting The Dark Into Spring

Through April's icy days
farmers burn dead branches
cut from orchards or scarred windbreaks.

The smoke of many fires
fills dark afternoons, drifts
over fields of frozen stubble.

Suddenly the deep frost leaves
and boys on bicycles race
along the rutted roads —

their shouts ignite the bonfire dusk.

Three Tiny Spring Poems

Near the creek
bur oak stand knee-deep
in their reflections.

At the millrace
shadows of dove and killdeer
touch cold water.

Fieldstone house –
martins nest
under dark eaves.

Spring Rain

Morning brings a dampness into the orchard. Throughout the woodlot, branches of northern hardwoods shine in their black skins. Early spring – faint green begins to outline the crowns of wild cherry and aspen. Maple blossoms, brought down last night, speckle the path.

The rain starts again, drifting in sheets across yard and pasture. I go down by the lake where silence has soaked into the beds where reeds sleep. In the lake's black corridors solitary fish seek the deepest spots. All day water falls into water.

Land fresh from the turning ploughs thickens with mud. Soon I can no longer be sure if this voice I hear belongs to the rain or the opened fields. When night advances from its house in the east, our sky becomes luminous like still waters deep in hidden wells or the first blood of a waking heart.

Two Pieces For Spring

By late April the rains cease;
rivers return to old channels
leaving pools that reflect
fresh green buds.

. .
. .

Under spring constellations
winds sweep the great oaks;
we walk near dark waters
with no need to speak.

The River In Early May

With the spring rains over, the Maitland settles lower between its banks to sing softly under the wings of migrating swallows. New leaves hesitate along branches that look down into the waters. Still, odd remnants of last year linger; brittle stalks of Queen Anne's Lace and common mullein stand between grey, glacial stones that embrace the spillway; seed-pods lie darkly among the roots of locusts.

Hand in hand, lovers already stroll through this first mild evening; sunset joins water and clouds, each an echo of the same lemon yellow, the same fading salmon. Life, so long locked within its fortress of ice, returns.

I feel no disappointment here, nor desire. Killdeer patrol the shallow pools; the whole cathedral sky opens its doors wide to moon and stars. In the village, house lights come on, each window throwing its bright square into the purple river.

May 10, 1994

For once the cardinal
falls silent

his furious mating stopped
by the daytime moon

as it cuts between
us and the sun

effortlessly swinging
ring of fire.

We watch the afternoon darken.

So simple an event
yet so rare

the day nearly perfect
almost cloudless —

the next time this happens
I'll be dead

even my youngest child
long grown up.

Return

Early in May a soft wind
slips unnoticed from the south
to set our forsythia free,
unlock the lavish magnolias
brimming pink and silver.

All over town
trees open their green day,
a flush creeps branch to branch
where warm sun breathes.

Wild grasses return from their knitted roots
as moisture rises
to find that level where
life begins.
          And suddenly I stand
gazing into the white
heart of spring.

Apple Tree In Spring

Completion comes
to the apple tree in spring.

The sun, closer now,
joins its shining hoop;

even my old glove,
lost so long ago,
returns.

The mountain of light
opens
          and every particle
flows out –
a river of silver
washing the blossoms

white to white
to rose.

The Apple

Spring becomes summer at a different moment each year. Although longed for, this transformation always comes as a surprise as if no one had anticipated it. When spring and summer are very early, this change can take place in mid-May, as it has this year. Already the last apple blossoms drift through my garden, their unhurried petals more delicate than whitest crêpe paper.

Lying at the base of the tree I watch slivers of light flash between young leaves as they move in the wind. Where the sun strikes bright, each leaf is outlined in sparkling white; boughs beyond boughs — every layer offers its unique shade of green to eyes long tired of winter's snow. Carpenter ants race along the trunk with a haste dictated by their important tasks.

I am content to stretch out on my back among blown petals which, now that fertilization has occurred, fall like snow through dense branches. An old tree already marked by rows of sapsucker scars, it bears well as hundreds of white flowers become sweet red fruit.

It is, of course, a rose and, like all members of its family, combines passion with knowledge. Grown only for eating, it's an unnatural hybrid. These trees exist in Midwestern Canada solely by the force of man's expanding will.

But that, like the rumoured garden of so long ago, is another poem. Today, only petals fall. They look exactly like those bits of airy paper tossed after a wedding. When the bride and her bridegroom have departed, all that remains is an empty street and a few dropped flowers touched, perhaps, by the faintest blush of pink.

With this in mind, I watch black insects rise in dark branches where all too soon ripe apples will form a string of lanterns lighting the harvest nights.

The Blossom Of The Yellow Pear

The blossom of the yellow pear opens five white petals to the May sun. Deep at its centre thin filaments thrust red tips into light as they complete their annual rites. Within their white house the anthers are rounded, sensuous with spring.

Behind these flowers, young leaves spread a luminous cloud, pale and fresh as the new season. The air fills with pollen when a breeze lifts laden branches to animate each radiant bloom in a tremble of delight. It is the slight trembling of water in my galvanized pail to the low murmur of a morning freight heading out for Detroit, hard steel wheels shaking clear liquid into a dance of concentric rings.

The whole earth lies open as it recreates itself under the touch of its nurturing sun. Around the pear's dark trunk, fiddle-heads unroll their green lace; the first wasp clings to my screen door. In the east, balconies of light overlook a swollen river where rafts of geese float. Green herons return to the wetlands along the edge of town, their *kew* ghosting among shadowed rushes.

And the bride enters the sanctuary on the arm of her father, her dress virginal like the pear in spring. She takes tiny steps, delicate and brimming with anticipation. Later, under a white moon, her body glows all night.

The Garden

The wind in the garden
wanders among fallen lilacs.

It comes like a dark whistle from night's hollow bone,
across plains where hands of wood
bury seeds while our moon hangs swollen.

Years pass
and I'm reminded of Nebraska –
how winter snows drift
thoughtlessly into the east.

Little by little my grief
is carried off,
is freed from its weight of stone flowers;

and I too wander
joyous at last
into the cold light
of stars.

Crawfish

Even in death the crawfish remains fierce, its armoured claws edged with a double row of yellow nodes and climaxing in points the colour of dried blood. The long, plated abdomen is gone, eaten by the predator along the river bank. The head and thorax form a torpedo, for the crawfish also lived the cunning life of a predator. There are two pairs of feelers; one set is short, resembling the riding crops of English huntsmen, the other long and flexible as bullwhips.

Ants have eaten the inside of its head; the delicate crawfish bones are fully exposed, and the raw necessity of the exoskeleton is apparent. Below the fierce exterior lies a vulnerability, hidden within the moist flesh, within the animal heart. How efficient the ants! Every shred of the living creature has been removed, converted into another life, now moving towards its own darkness.

And in that shadow the crawfish must have turned – for the claws are raised, extended – must have faced the raccoon on that final night of unequal struggle. It must have realized at last the undeniable fact of its own brief life, its short passage through the mundane realm, through the day-to-day chores of living.

The sun sinks lower. Finally, I understand the crawfish has become ecstatic. Free of this life, claws held high, it dances along the edge of a river that gathers the night to give birth to our next, fleeting day.

Northern Trains

Deep in the quiet hours
unseen locomotives call.

I hear them lonely
beyond my garden's black cloak,

lonely throughout the nights
of small dark towns.

They whistle along an Ontario Northland spur
where summer opens

like the mouth of a child
already learning to say goodbye.

Indigo Bunting

The indigo bunting
        is a flash of blue
iridescent among new leaves
   where the path verges
        on cool water.

His flight moves like blue flame
        through shadows so dense
the river's voice
   barely pierces
        their green silence.

The Taste

A morning so fresh the sun shines like
a school of minnows flashing through pure water.
My daughter climbs a willow; small bare toes
grip bark ridged and furrowed with age.

Later, Simone wades that moist edge
where land becomes lake. She chases baby catfish
through cool shallows, her world instant and direct,
each moment luminous with her joy or anger.

Lunch time comes. Across a wooden bench we spread
cheese, oranges, bread, and wine.
On the back of my tongue a single crimson drop
recalls the hand-worked cask.

I taste oak staves, hours of sunlight,
the dusky shadows of vines where vineyards run down
to the sea. The wine holds a sharp fruitiness
tossed, like a child's laughter, fresh in the mouth.

Brim

Kingfishers flash away and back
a wing-beat above this pond
swollen with last night's downpour.

Year of freakish summer rains;
creeks overflow into fields
their rich mud swamping the young corn.

My daughter naps on a blanket that once was mine.
Not far away, a muskrat patrols
the brim of her watery world.

Baby, man, muskrat —
our very world passes away
in a blink, in an instant.

Willows weep into the pond,
their branches deep in the risen waters
where green and its green echo are one.

Simone At The River

All season the sun pours
its light into the Thames.
Carp feed and grow
to crest in a world of reeds and silt.

And crested they surge from cool mud
to flicker golden on the surface.
They pass like silent flames
through blue shadows
and are gone.

Your face as you look
into the river's wet dark
is also golden.
It's a child face,
precious beyond measure.

Out of your mouth
come shining words –

     "Fish"
          "Water"
               "Swim"

– fleeting as flecks
    of sunlight
where the waters lie wrapped
in their blue layers.

Inside The Stone

A grey boulder, rounded by the Maitland, yields a purple shell when smashed on the river bank. Almost like amethyst, but duller, the shell has remained surrounded by its prison of stone since the late Silurian. Lying among weeds its hue matches the leaves of wild carrot, purpled by frost.

The hollow of the shell is filled with sediment, hardened by heat and time. This is the cavity where life once lived, ecstatic and free. This animal, too, is preserved: a mineral tongue locked in its silent vault. Once opened the rock smells like the sea, or like the bride shy in her marriage bed: salty, ready for the dark shadow to enter her loneliness and make it whole. And when the bride cries out in the night, what good will it do us who cannot know if she cries in pain or joy?

As the days grow shorter, we pull smooth stones from cold water to build a dam. Our labour is hard – a service to our community. Yet we cannot follow the woman on her journey. Her goal is the dark of the mountain – the side furthest from man – and she must travel alone. In her arms she carries a gift of light, like the moon rising from the ocean.

When the bride returns, decades later, her womb filled with life, we will have grown old, our work unended. Only then will she go to her husband's house and place in his trembling hands the fossil of a shell.

Quarry

At the centre
of a cornfield
lies a gravel deposit;

smoothed rocks
hidden by a glacier
twenty thousand years ago.
Place where

our land's stone heart
is laid bare to the
empty sky;

where at dusk
clouds and mist return
to their haven
under the earth.

Grape Vine

Dark green and veined like the back of a hand, grape leaves catch the patch of light that has tumbled through the boughs of this spreading cottonwood. Hungry for sunlight, filled with a blind desire to ascend, wild grape tendrils grasp a young buckthorn. And, wildly stringy, the vines climb stray shafts of light toward that distant hole in the canopy left when one or two great branches fell during last autumn's storms.

Even now, the vine's survival is not secured; should it continue to stretch branch by branch into the sky, it will learn the pain of light, will twist and knot, binding that darkness where past and future merge. Then its bark will take on a tough coarseness, become an old man's skin – splintery and dry.

The wild grape drags its long, snaking body higher through the buckthorn; still it is never enough. The thirst for the sun grows as the vine grows. The old men are silent; they know they watch a dance where only one can live. By now their bark hides all the soft, vulnerable fibres. It is harsh, like the armour of a snapping turtle concealed deep within a muskrat lodge.

The sap also has its hidden sorrow . . . a pale, sugary taste known only through sacrifice. On summer afternoons, boys stand beneath the severed vines to trap, with eager tongues, the drops of darkness falling.

Midsummer Eve

After lovemaking
    the wind enters
the dark heart
       of the aspens,
Heaven's River
    summons a new season.

A Door In The Water

Across miles of cornfields
we come at last to a lake where
the blue of a Midwest sky
enters the darker blue
of deep waters.

Everywhere lies the still hand
of summer, the sweep
of space without measure.
Footstep by footstep
we leave the details of our world.

In the yellowing tassels
a time of mourning. In the
breeze through the arched leaves
the sound of mystery.
Far to the west, beyond the

mountains we cannot see,
the sun flames. Mountains
greater than mountains.
Under a salmon sky
we open the door to the water.

In Country Sweat

Pure summer; the timothy stands
tall in its shadows
at a field's dark border
where a few spikes were left standing
after the mowing.

Stomach to stomach
we move locked in country sweat
towards that glistening instant
when our world is lost in joy.
Only the heat remains,

and that dog barking
behind his high gate.
Within the eaves' afternoon dusk
we cling breathless as friction
closes the lock of our flesh.

Nightfall In Sturgeon Bay Marsh

Passing through the marsh at dusk
I watch our sun outline each blade of grass
as it slips west at day's blue end.

Crickets swell with song; mute swans
arch great wings over dark waters.
Shadows fill the beds where cattails sleep.

The sands curve eastward, and Long Point
rides on Erie's currents, moves
beneath the sway of transitory birds.

Silent stars descend. Walking
wet sand at midnight, I step into
that stillpoint where lake and night are one.

Triptych

Heartland

Crickets slowly fill the night
with slivers of the moon.
I watch a tree outside my window
draw life from our living earth.
The soil trembles and still
people keep coming: American refugees,
the hungry Irish, that long
dark line of escaped slaves.

Each carries a thimble of fire.
Each measures his world
with the feathers of a sparrow.
Midsummer. White stars cast down salt
to fill the caves of the heart.
In this season of witches
water cries out from the clear
wells at dawn.

The Map Of The Midwest

When the harvest comes
friction turns
corn to lightning;

rain falls darkly
through wounded cottonwoods,
scattering branches

to the black earth.
Unfolding a map
of the Midwest

I see its net of roads,
cities I have never
visited.

I am a foreigner
yet, in an odd way,
have always lived here.

The thunder lighting up
the shattered sky
rolls a thousand miles.

Autumn Returns

A day drunk on yellow
tumbles from the clear sky.
Carp rise slowly
the black river
filling their mouths.

Across the floodplain
loosestrife and goldenrod
bend under a clamour
of migrating birds
their songs lost on the wind.

Bewildered Loyalists advance
beating the air with iron bells.
Generations later
their voices retain
an American flatness

cut with harsh intolerance,
with their abiding fear.
In these Midwest fields
pale bones float
brittle in the harvest cold.

In Harvest Quiet

Woodstock floats
on a sea of goldenrod
broken only by asters
scattered along a railway cut.

The flowers are blue shadow
like that hawk
circling the elevators,
or the blur of a passing freight.

When the harvest is finished
implements are shut away –
the scent of barn dust,
machine oil, lingers.

It is then a sharpness
drifts in on the Prairie wind
and glides like a raptor
suspended at sunset

midway between
the thin pale blue of heaven
and our darkening smoke-blue earth,
waiting to fall.

Timesweep

Fingers of rain
slip in off Lake Huron
to cloak my garden,
hiding potatoes, garlic, those slim green onions
within a web of mist.
Concord grapes ripen with a slow blush.

Everywhere the mystery continues.
People die or fade to nothing,
old streets
                change,
plywood covers rows of schoolroom windows
where once
sunlight stained an afternoon yellow.

Milkweed and thistle
spread out from along a WPA wall,
replace a knotted yew
that used to guard
the flagpole.

Already autumn patterns this Midwest town;
red leaves
spot and fall from sugar maples.
In steady rain
waves of clouds break
when rivers speak.

A White Egret

for Gerry Shikatani

Part I

1

Dried-up edge of lake
    or pond

dried-up   cracked
  on top

yet wet below
  grey clay

2

Beyond the mud
common egret

    alert

3

I sink deep

break through
  this dry crust
  to my knees

4

At the border
of land and water

maple, poplar
 red
    yellow

autumn clouds pile up

Part II

1

A dense marl
at the foot
  of the cliff

this constant grey

2

Layer after layer

built up
  like language

3

People drift across the land
  words spoken

voiced

     in which
  meaning adheres

Part III

1

A graceful white bird
wading shallow water

just beyond
    the edge

2

Perhaps three feet tall
common along ponds
salt & fresh-water marshes

and mudflats

3

Since the last ice age

clay from these cliffs
washed down
       built up

layer after layer
like generations of
  egrets

Part IV

1

Clumsy in thick mud
such noise I make!

The egret
        alert
is frightened

2

Rich lowlands
of the Great Lakes Basin

water / land
run together

  I ponder
the meaning of these
            great white birds

3

Against the sky
        the powerful wings

arc clear.

First Light

Aspens appear from autumn mists
their boughs yellowing
under northern clouds.

The sound of a creek
still hidden in darkness
comes through the open window.

We lie quietly in bed
enwrapped by the coolness
of early dawn.

Three Small Poems For Autumn

After twenty years
my thoughts still return home
        with the autumn wind.

Valley of the Conestogo:
the river a blue scar
        through cleared fields.

Under a crown of crows
the maple lights
        the whole sky.

Homage To Carl Sandburg

Autumn Numbers

In late September
a coolness comes on the night wind
turning the first maples to gold.

        .   .

        .   .

    The rushbeds stand silent
    where mallards hid bright families
    among curved green shadows.

            .   .

            .   .

        Across this heartland of red silk corn
        slow rivers draw a deeper blue
        from the autumn sky.

                .   .

                .   .

            Almost at midnight,
            almost overhead –
            the ghost-light of Andromeda
            falls through two million years.

Ferns

Ferns dance on the wind along a split-log fence.
They keep spring's slow green throughout the furnace
        days of summer when flares of sunlight flick
        between the boughs of sugar maples.

Even in the relentless heat the ferns are a cool
        thought holding the memory of spring.
Under the shadows of spreading trees they think and
        dream that dark scent of moist earth piled high
        behind the turning ploughs.

Lament

Under a half-moon
the city is a shifting patchwork
of quicksilver shadows
strung on a Prairie wind.

Long into the night's pale hours
the wind repeats the corn's dry song
of fields bleached
by sharp harvest skies.

The voice in the stalks
is a lament born of
that flat land beyond
the Mississippi. Like a dark river

it reaches through the night
and goes quietly leaving
a yellow silence where
darkness pools and runs.

October Sunday At The Cove

I

Maple and oak stain the water red;
I watch their colour shift
around the still surfaces of stones
where a dry creek enters the cove.

II

All afternoon things happen around me:
small animals I can never see
root in fallen leaves; fish leap
from their dark homes below.

III

I do nothing but sit quietly
while hidden lives rise
and fall about me. The heron
has yet to follow the kingfishers south.

IV

We must meet hidden travellers
wherever we journey. The cove is dead calm.
From within God's blue silence
an osprey's piercing call.

Staghorn

Into the chill of an October sky
this sumac casts its scarlet heart.

Iridescent leaves light cold fields
where beaten stubble mixes with pale grass.

Its limbs are a bonfire set by
the numb white fingers of an early frost.

Brants

On a crook
            of blue water

small black geese
         pause
in their migration

            to the Chesapeake.

They float
            where cold currents
         dive
through shadows
            of cut-bank vines.

Brants dot
            the autumn river
as it flows
   among reeds

         and
            the season's
                  first frost.

The River In Early October

The river, which had been slow and shallow all summer, runs fuller now, its waters dark and fast. Bits of foam rush downstream as if the call of the autumn sea grew stronger each day. Long grasses, their stalks deep in the risen liquid, are yellow where the river cuts a wide curve through a pasture with two white mares.

For the first time in months the scent of woodsmoke drifts sharp through still air. The river has shaken the sloth of summer; a red leaf falls to the surface to be immediately swept into the swirling descent.

Everything moves lower; bulrushes, burdened with the season, bend toward their roots; the sap retreats in trees that overhang the bank. In its own way the yellow birch welcomes this changed mood, relinquishing thousands of leaves to the same downward motion, urgently and without regret. And the cherries have long abandoned most of their leaves; they flee like adolescents eager to leave home for the city.

When evening comes, moisture rises from the surface. These vapours, white in white moonlight, ignore the movements of the river despite being almost within its wet embrace. By midnight only two things remain: the mist, still lingering among sedges, and the sound of darkness descending into this world of matter and loss.

James Deahl was born in Pittsburgh at the close of World War II and grew up among the hills and rivers of western Pennsylvania and West Virginia.

Most of the pieces in this, his thirteenth poetry title, were written during the five years he lived in London, Ontario. While in London, he was keenly interested in the United Empire Loyalists and their legacy, still present throughout rural Ontario.

He currently lives in Hamilton, Ontario, with his wife Gilda and his two youngest daughters, Simone and Shona. After many years as a full-time writer, Deahl presently works in horticulture, earning the greater part of his living twirling the tendrils of passion flowers.

In 1996 he was presented with the Award of Excellence by the Hamilton & Region Arts Council for his work in poetry.

Poetry by James Deahl

In The Lost Horn's Call, 1982
Steel Valley (with Bruce Meyer and Gilda Mekler),1984
No Cold Ash, 1984
Blue Ridge, 1985
Into This Dark Earth (with Raymond Souster), 1985
A Stand Of Jackpine (with Milton Acorn), 1987
Geschriebene Bilder, 1990
Opening The Stone Heart, 1992
Heartland, 1993
Even This Land Was Born Of Light, 1993
Tasting The Winter Grapes, 1995
Blackbirds, 1999

Prose by James Deahl

Real Poetry, 1981
The Future of Poetry: Despair or Joy?, 1991
The Andromeda Factor, 1991
Under The Watchful Eye, 1995
Poetry Markets for Canadians, sixth edition, 1996

Edited by James Deahl

The Uncollected Acorn (Milton Acorn), 1987
I Shout Love and Other Poems (Milton Acorn), 1987
The Northern Red Oak: Poems for and About Milton Acorn, 1987
Hundred Proof Earth (Milton Acorn), 1988
Let the Earth Take Note, 1994
The Road to Charlottetown (Milton Acorn & Cedric Smith), 1998
The Saving Bannister, 2000

Other poetry titles by Unfinished Monument Press, hamilton haiku press, and Mekler & Deahl, Publishers

Milton Acorn, **To Hear the Faint Bells:**
    haiku, senryu, and short poems from Canada's national poet
Milton Acorn and James Deahl, **A Stand of Jackpine**
Milton Acorn and Cedric Smith, **The Road to Charlottetown**
Becky D. Alexander (editor), **Paradise Poems:** *haiku from Cootes Paradise*
Herb Barrett, **The Light Between**
Fred Cogswell (judge), **Doors of the Morning:** *The Sandburg-Livesay Award, 1996*
James Deahl, **Blackbirds**
James Deahl (editor), **Mix Six**
James Deahl (editor), **The Northern Red Oak:** *poems for and about Milton Acorn*
Chris Faiers and Mark McCawley (editors), **Small Press Lynx:**
    An Anthology of Small Press Writers
Simon Frank, **Imaginary Poems**
LeRoy Gorman (editor), **Gathering Light:** *The Herb Barrett Award, 1996*
Albert W.J. Harper, **Poems of Reflection**
Hans Jongman (editor), **Sweeping Leaves:** *The Herb Barrett Award, 1999*
John B. Lee, **The Echo of Your Words Has Reached Me**
Tanis MacDonald, **This Speaking Plant:** *The Acorn-Rukeyser Award, 1996*
Joy Hewitt Mann, **grass:** *The Acorn-Rukeyser Award, 1999*
Judge Mazebedi, **Chicken Cries Out**
Walt Peterson, **In the Waiting Room of the Speedy Muffler King:**
    The Acorn-Rukeyser Award, 1998
Ted Plantos (editor), **Not to Rest in Silence:** *A celebration of people's poetry*
Anna Plesums, **Intrinsic Revelations**
Anna Plesums, **Love and Words**
Al Purdy (judge), **Sing for the Inner Ear:** *The Sandburg Livesay Award, 1997*
Kay Redhead, **The Song of the Artichoke Lover**
Linda Rogers, **Picking the Stones:** *The Acorn-Rukeyser Award, 1997*
Margaret Saunders (editor), **Cold Morning:** *The Herb Barrett Award, 1997*
Joanna C. Scott, **Coming Down from Bataan:** *The Acorn-Rukeyser Award, 2000*
Jeff Seffinga, **Bailey's Mill**
Jeff Seffinga (editor), **A Cliff Runs Through It**
Jeff Seffinga (editor), **Ingots**
Jeff Seffinga, **Tight Shorts:** *haiku and other short poems*
Raymond Souster (judge), **No Choice But to Trust**: *The Sandburg-Livesay Award, 1999*
Michael Dylan Welch (editor), **Through the Spirea:** *The Herb Barrett Award, 1998*
Jim C. Wilson (judge), **Waiting for You to Speak:** *The Sandburg-Livesay Award, 1998*

Unfinished Monument Press was founded in 1978 by Chris Faiers. Under his leadership, the press published 36 poetry collections. Mekler & Deahl took over the press in 1995 and has continued to emphasize people's poetry. Authors published during the press's first 15 years include Milton Acorn, Shaunt Basmajian, jwcurry, James Deahl, Chris Faiers, Mona Fertig, Marshall Hryciuk, Bruce Hunter, (Daniel) Jones, Mark McCawley, Robert Priest, Wayne Ray, Margaret Saunders, and Raymond Souster.